GLYN GOODE

Pictures in the

SAND

POEMS OF CONTEMPLATION

GLYN GOODE

Pictures in the SAND

POEMS OF CONTEMPLATION

MEMOIRS
Cirencester

Published by Memoirs

MEMOIRS
PUBLISHING

1A The Wool Market, Dyer Street, Cirencester, Gloucestershire, GL7 2PR
info@memoirsbooks.co.uk www.memoirspublishing.com

Pictures in the Sand: Poems of Contemplation

ISBN: 978-1-86151-048-8

To my daughters Stephanie and Nicole and my son Christian.

You are my World.

TABLE OF CONTENTS

THE PROPOSAL

NICOLE

GONE MISSING

BY YOUR SIDE

A FRIEND IN NEED

TIME FOR A REST

STEPHANIE

ST. MICHAEL'S MOUNT
KERNOW

ONE WAY TICKET

PEN PAL

FAINT HEARTED

SECOND SIGHT

ODE TO ANNIE

WRONG

UNTETHERED

DOWN AND OUT

GONE FISHING

BURP

QUESTIONS BUT NO
ANSWERS

CHRISTMAS IN NEVER-NEVER
LAND

MEMO

HEALTH AND SAFETY

CHANGE TACT

DESPAIR

JOB SATISFACTION

I AM YOU

MY NUMBER IS

LEARNING CURVE

AND HERE IS THE NEWS

DETOUR

BLOOD BROTHERS

SALVATION

KARMA

UNSUNG HEROES

PEACE OF MIND

CARE BEAR	A BIT OF WHAT YOU FANCY
CHRISTIAN	SOUNDLESS
OVERDRAWN	WHAT IF IT RAINS?
SKY LARK	MY GATE
LEAVING HOME	EDUCATION
HAPPINESS	AUTUMN IN JUNE
END OF THE RAINBOW	NEVER GIVE UP
HOLIDAYS	LAST FLING
HOME ALONE	FANTASY
ONE STEP AT A TIME	TUNELESS
NIGHT OWLS	FOORPRINTS IN THE SAND
LE ESCARGOT	A DARKENED ROOM
SOWING THE SEEDS	WAITING IN THE WINGS
ONCE	DERAILED
SILENTLY CALL	A STRANGER CAME CALLING
HOP SKIP AND JUMP	LAZY MIND
IGNORANCE IS BLISS	UNISON
FEBRUARY 3rd	OH BOY
BELIEVE	HAPPILY POOR
AGAINST ALL ODDS	THE OLD CODGER
SINGLE PARENT	ALLOTMENT
GARBAGE 24/7	CUL DE SAC
CHILL OUT	A DISTANT HORIZON
TIDAL	NATURE'S GIFT
POSITIVE THINKING	WASH YOUR HANDS AFTER HANDLING
KNOW YOUR FRIENDS	
	BARMAID

HONEY

NO HUGS

THE FORGETFUL POET

ANTHEM

LOVING WORDS

NIGHT CHILLS

FREE AT LAST

FEATHERBRAIN

NO RESPITE

DISH OF THE DAY

SECOND TIME AROUND

FINALE

CATASTROPHIC

HOPE SPRINGS ETERNAL

ITCHY FEET

NO HARD FEELINGS

A REAL JOY

ALWAYS

BLACK COFFEE

UNFORGIVING

EXCURSION

WELCOME TO THE REAL WORLD

SLEEPLESS

LOST AND FOUND

DAMSELFLY

BLUSHING

REFLECTIONS

A NEVER-ENDING LOVE

BEST FRIEND

A REFRESHING BREEZE

MEDIUM RARE

WORLD THRO' MY EYES

POLITICAL PRISONER

A TICKING CLOCK

WHAT IF?

FATAL EXTRACTION

REVEAL ALL

HOT AND HUMID

NOT OF THIS WORLD

A COOL REFRESHING DRINK

MORNING VISITORS

NOT OUT

TOO HARD

AU REVOIR

THE PROPOSAL

You have the scent of a rose
Such a lithe elegant pose
Your voice is so sweet
Like a songbird calling to meet
Your complexion is strawberries and cream
You are my ideal, my dream
So witty and funny
Adorable like an Easter Bunny
You are the joy of my life
Please be my wife?

NICOLE

My dearest daughter Nicole
I love you with all my heart and soul
I love you more each day
More than words could ever say
You make the stars twinkle at night
You fill my heart with delight

I am here to share your fears
Wipe away your tears
Because you're so gentle and kind
With a beautiful mind
Such a beautiful face
You are all elegance and grace.

GONE MISSING

You go to catch the bus
Get in the queue
You don't make a fuss
Then you wait and wait
The bus is late
The timetable is all the talk
I don't bother to use the bus now
It's quicker to walk.

BY YOUR SIDE

I know you are so angry and sad
With the violence shown by your dad
Your mind is engulfed by a swirling tide
But you are strong enough to turn it aside
Your feelings you don't have to hide
For I am here for you, by your side
You are a young girl so beautiful
With the whole world in front of you
You don't have to have any fears
For you will have many happy years.

A FRIEND IN NEED

We all need an incentive
A reason to live
We all need someone who will care
Who will be there
Someone who will come around
Lift you up when you're down
A shoulder to lean on and cry
Someone who won't walk by.

TIME FOR A REST

I need to take time to sleep
Away from this world that makes me weep
A world that is corrupt and rotten
A world that God has forgotten.

STEPHANIE

You are one of a kind
Sweet daughter of mine
Your smile is brighter than the sun
You are so bubbly and full of fun
As the day gets longer
My love for you grows stronger

If you need help in your career
You know I am always here
You talk with a soft sigh
Like a white cloud drifting by
Always a smile on your beautiful face
A frown would be out of place.

ST. MICHAEL'S MOUNT KERNOW

Thro' my window I look out
Across the bay to St. Michael's Mount
With its turrets on high
Reaching for the sky
It's an icon of the ages
History written on its pages
Stroll across the causeway
On a warm spring day
Feel the history enclose you like a glove
Past hatred, past love
Tall and majestic it stands
Guardian of a proud land.

ONE WAY TICKET

All my life I've been alone
Nowhere to call home
People I thought were friends
Just used me for their own ends
When all is said and done
I've been used, just for fun
There's only one being I've met
That treated me with respect.

I'm going on a journey very soon
Once the sun has passed the moon
To his spirit in the sky
To my Ben on high.

PEN PAL

Sitting at my table thinking
All I've got is my writing
A lot of my thoughts are despondent
You my reader are my only correspondent.

FAINT HEARTED

I'm waiting for the night
To block out the light
That's bearing down on me
Leaving me naked for all to see
My thoughts are my own
Seeds that I have sown
Don't need to hear your song
To know right from wrong
I don't need to wait around
For long ago I found
Fate will soon tear you apart
If you arc mcek of heart.

SECOND SIGHT

The wind moves the clouds aside
My doubts they can no longer hide
The tide is now turning for me
Pictures in the sand I can now see
Images from my past
Now long gone at last
The future I can now see is bright
Now I've gained second sight.

ODE TO ANNIE

When your emotions are down to zero
And you are looking for a hero
You need my friend Annie
A loving mother and grannie
She will take in any waif or stray
That may come her way
She will give them all a home
A rest from their endless roam.

But she has nothing to gain
Tho' her own life is filled with pain
She gives out so much love
A true angel from above
A beautiful woman with a heart of gold
Such a treasure, a delight to behold.

UNTETHERED

Cold is the falling rain
A river of ice thro' my vein
Blood turned into water
Emotions sent for the slaughter
Many years I've strived
To keep our love alive
But you were at my throat
As if I was a sacrificial goat
But the tether has now been broken
The mouse has now awoken
For the hunted has now turned hunter
I say to you beware the thunder.

WRONG

I loved you
Didn't know how to say
Thought I showed you
In my own way.

DOWN AND OUT

When you are alone
Without a home
Out on the street
With no one to meet
Words come into your head
Never to be read
Thoughts that wither in the wind
Never to be seen
With no one to care
Your emotions you cannot share
Alone you shed your tears
No one to share your fears
For you soon found
Your tears fell on stony ground.

GONE FISHING

I know I squirm
But I'm only a little worm
Wriggling in the earth
For all I'm worth
I'm often to be found
Fertilising the ground
But it won't last, knowing my luck
I'll end up on an angler's hook
I don't deserve this
Being swallowed by a fish!

BURP

The anaconda is a massive snake
I watched it swimming across the lake
Ever closer to the shore
Its hunger it cannot ignore
A woman at the shore taking drinks
It's safe here, she thinks
It wraps itself around her
Then drags her down under
Crushes and swallows the silly cow
I don't care, don't love her anymore anyhow.

QUESTIONS BUT NO ANSWERS

It was a summer morn
When our love was born
I gave you a kiss on the cheek
Young children so naive and meek
We would walk hand in hand
Innocent love so grand
We went to separate schools
In those days they were the rules

We couldn't bear to be apart
Oh, be still, my aching heart
Walking down the path to church
Thinking, don't leave me in the lurch
But it was fine, we were wed
Many a tear was shed
We had a lovely home
Just the two of us home alone

But then you had to work away from home
Didn't see you often but we spoke on the phone
Then I received the letter
Thought I knew you better
I suppose the life we led
Would bring us to this watershed
When it's all said and done
You really don't know someone

I found my life was torn apart
That letter was a knife thro' my heart
Now I walk down the path towards the gate
Thinking, is it now too late?
I look back to our home across the lawn
Thro' the mist of early dawn
Questions race through my mind
But no answers can I find.

MEMO

It's worth making a note
Death is just a tote
It doesn't come by rõte
It wears a varied coat.

CHRISTMAS IN NEVER-NEVER LAND

It's that time of year again
When people go completely insane
Loads of presents they must find
We've got no money but never mind
We may not be rich
But we've got loads of plastic
We've got no money to pay our debt
But hey, what the heck!

Shopping trolleys overflowing with food
Most of which will never be used
Next year it will be the same again
Continuing this mindless trend
It should be a time of prayer and hymn
Not turned commercially into complete mayhem
But will it change? – no fear
They all start again to bring in the New Year.

HEALTH AND SAFETY

Seeing the stars above
Reminds me of you, my love
They are shining and bright
As you are at night
With all your charm
You do my heart harm.

CHANGE TACT

And now it's time
To clear my mind
Wipe away the tear
Prepare for the New Year
No more sugar and spice
You get nowhere being nice
No more just and fair
Now more like a grizzly bear.

DESPAIR

I know a young girl
Whose mind is in a terrible whirl
In an endless surging tide
She cannot turn aside
But her pain is my pain
For I've been there, can't return again
I will help cure her despair
Because I love her and care
I will not let her mind be scarred
Or her life be marred
Together, she will pull thro' this
That is my fervent wish.

JOB SATISFACTION

Some of my poems are very deep
Thoughts I could no longer keep
But some thoughts I think I share
There are others who have no one to care
If my words help just one person
I will consider my job done
If I can make someone again smile
My life will have been worthwhile.

I AM YOU

I am a speck of sand
That falls thro' your hand
An element floating in space
A tiny speck before your face
But wait, there is more
I'm a sliver of ore
And that is not all that's left
For I am very deft
There is more than you think
I am the water that you drink
You are part atom
That's where I come from
You are part bone
But you are not alone
You are oxygen and carbon
For we are one.

MY NUMBER IS

Nothing left to say
Going to call it a day
I think I've said it all
Just waiting for the call.

LEARNING CURVE

They say you learn with age
Oh please turn the page
You just become full of rage
Like a tiger prowling his cage
You want to pull out your hair
Because you cannot climb the stair
All you do when you get older
Is think of what you did when you
were younger
So you are knowledgeable with age
Pity you are a knackered old sage.

AND HERE IS THE NEWS

What a horrible world we live in
All violence and sin
It's all blood and gore
I can't take this anymore
All the news is black
Will happiness ever come back?
I need a place in the sun
Just relax and have some fun
No e-mail or mobile phone
I need a news-free zone.

DETOUR

Waiting at the traffic light
Motor purring but things don't seem right
I've been down this road before
Not going there anymore
She wants me as her lover
But I belong to another
I've got to turn around
For I'm duty bound
This situation is perverse
Clutch in, engage reverse.

BLOOD BROTHERS

We have been friends for many a year
Had some laughs, shed many a tear
But before my time is up and I go
I just want you to know
Our friendship was by blood bound
And don't forget you owe me Twenty Pound.

SALVATION

I was a young man carrying a heavy load
Walking down a lonely endless road
Love had missed my address so it seems
Then I bumped into the girl of my dreams
Shyly I help her to her feet
Fate states this is how we would meet
The first touch of her hand
And my emotions were bound
She has the brightest eyes I've ever seen
A sparkling luminous emerald green
When I was down and needing love
An angel appeared from above.

KARMA

It's catching you up fast
Your long lost past
Your mind is troubled now
But you know somehow
There's only one place you want to be
That's here next to me
Turn your negative emotions aside
Take that bus, enjoy the ride.

UNSUNG HEROES

Bombs fall from darkened skies
Like a swarm of flies
No cathedrals left to enthral
Everything's gone, nothing left at all.

Thro' ruined buildings and rubble
The unsung heroes stumble
Faces covered in grime
Time after time
Onward and ever forward they go
Into the face of a ferocious foe
No thought of turning back
Courage they do not lack.

I feel so tiny, so small
For me they gave their all
They made the ultimate sacrifice
For me they gave their life
Though they are now gone
Their memory lives on
Thro' the soul of my mind
Their spirit I can find.

*Dedicated to the men and women of the
United Kingdom's Armed Forces.*

Thank You.

PEACE OF MIND

Alone in the house again
Heart wracked by pain
Waiting for the phone to sound
Once again make my heart pound
But it's the cold wind of despair
That now blows thro' my hair,
These feelings in my heart
Are tearing me apart
I need to sort out my head
Some things are best left unsaid
So much hurt in my mind
Peace I need to find.

CARE BEAR

I am the bear
Big shoulders to cry on
Someone who will care
A person you can rely on.

CHRISTIAN

You are so much like me
We both love Rugby
Whether it's league or union
It's our shared passion
Can't understand tho' why you're so tall
And I am so small
Is it because in my teens
I wore tight jeans
But you are a special loving man
You are my one and only son, my Christian.

OVERDRAWN

I have been asked what is love
It would be easier to touch the stars above
Is it the sudden loss of appetite?
Or the long restless night
Walking around in a hypnotic state
Doing things you really hate
Or is it the letter that you dread
Telling you your account is in the red?
Is it the loss of concentration?
This is an unanswerable question.

SKY LARK

She is the lark singing in the sky
A fluffy white cloud drifting by
She has sweet little mischievous ways
Her smile brightens cold winter days
A spirit that is wild and free
She is my beautiful daughter Stephanie.

LEAVING HOME

My world revolves around you
You are everything I think and do
You are every beat of my heart
But one day I know we will part
You will always be my life and soul
My sweetest daughter Nicole.

HAPPINESS

Four words that I love to hear
Words that bring me cheer
Four words that make my heart glad
'I love you dad.'

END OF THE RAINBOW

I've lived my life on a wing and prayer
Here, there, and everywhere
No thought of tomorrow
Just me and my old friend sorrow
Jump in feet first
Then in the morning cursed
My life was a complete mess
Then I turned up in Skegness.

Things just seemed to get worse
Then I met you, my nurse
Now you're wearing my ring
You never know what life will bring.

HOLIDAYS

I thought your absence would never end
You're my daughter, my best friend
I've missed you so much
But I'm glad you kept in touch.

HOME ALONE

Now you are singing a different song
Please tell me what I have done wrong
There must be a reason
For your treason
Oh, the day I rue
Of being faithful to you
Black clouds are all I can see
Rain is now falling on me
Here I am all alone
You've gone, no one home.

ONE STEP AT A TIME

Days in the park
With your girl, have a lark
Long summer days of fun
Basking in the sun
You give her a tentative kiss
Your heart gives a miss
You hug each other and cuddle
Minds in a confusing muddle
You are both in a rush
It's young love's first flush.

NIGHT OWLS

In the dark of night
There are things to give you fright
Creatures that creep and stir
Leave your mind in a whirl
Things you don't want to meet
Because they want you to eat.

If you're a little mouse, be wary
For things can get very scary
So don't give a reason to grieve
Hide now under the leaves.

LE ESCARGOT

So you are a little snail
That's no reason to wail
It's a slow path you tread
But you have a roof over your head
So you feel you are hated
Hunted and baited
If you leave our vegetables alone
We will leave you free to roam.

SOWING THE SEEDS

Life for all is the same
It's just a game
But the rich have different rules
They treat the poor as fools
But this is not wise
For the poor will rise
It's all part of evolution
The people will have their revolution.

ONCE

Swirling clouds, mist of grey
Thro' my mind another day
Dying daffodils in long grass
There for all to pass
Adders weaving to and fro
Another avenue for me to go
Cloud breaking for sun to shine
She was once a love of mine.

SILENTLY CALL

I am here, can't you see
I call, can't you hear me?
Want to talk to you
But I don't know how to
Never felt like this before
Don't know what's in store
So I just pass you by
Oh, how I curse being shy.

HOP SKIP AND JUMP

He was only having a lark
An amusing little aardvark
No need for silly little rants
Because you've got ants in your pants
You shouldn't have stood still
Next to a giant ant hill.

IGNORANCE IS BLISS

Still waters run deep
Dark secrets to keep
Some things best left unsaid
In the graveyard dead
Be warned, don't pry
Truth will only make you cry.

FEBRUARY 3RD

Today is your day
Remembered in a special way
Always I'm thinking of you
In everything I do
Without you I am lost
But no matter what the cost
Your going will not be in vain
For we will be together again.

BELIEVE

My mind I need to clear
Your voice I want to hear
This is a very strange place
No image of your face
All I needed was you
No one else would do
Might as well leave now
No point in life somehow
But wait, I will come thro'
There's more to life than you.

AGAINST ALL ODDS

Young woman never wanted a child
The thought drove her wild
So she took the contraceptive pill
But then against her will
A little sperm slipped thro' a gap
Into her womb and took a nap.

In her mind was a terrible thought
This baby I have to abort
But then she backed away
And so, here I am today.

SINGLE PARENT

I pass you by on the street
My eyes you will not meet
You were my wife
The love of my life
The children miss you
But I don't know what to do
If you had a soul
It would be blacker than coal
Wish we had never met
So why do I still fret?

GARBAGE 24/7

Looking at the television screen
Thinking, all this I've seen
Programmes that are supposed to be funny
A complete waste of money
Wildlife programmes I've seen before
Now a complete bore.

Television companies just cheat
Everything is a constant repeat
No one has any new ideas
All they have are fears
Frightened to try new stuff
Just keep our jobs, that's good enough.

CHILL OUT

So you're carrying a bug
Well, you *are* a slug
You really take your time
Your path is covered in slime
You give yourself a bad name
For gardeners' you are fair game.
Take time out for a while
Feel the breeze and smile.

TIDAL

I look out to sea
The horizon's closing in on me
There's a surge in the tide
My feelings I can no longer hide
Deep within my soul I look
Scattered pages torn from a book
Need to lift this sense of dismay
Return from the dark of yesterday
Turn my back on this blight
Open the door of daylight
Love you have to earn
One day the tide will turn.

POSITIVE THINKING

If you close your mind to today
Your hurt will go away
It will all seem like a dream
Washed away by a stream
Don't have thoughts that are negative
You will get your wish, just be positive.

KNOW YOUR FRIENDS

There's no breeze, the night is still
In my room there's an unearthly chill
This is not a night to be out
For there is absolute evil about
It will leave your mind in a deadly whirl
Enough to make your blood curl.
If strangers come and call
For their charms do not fall
They will be friendly for a while
But don't wait until they smile
For this is not a time to panic
Hold your cross, throw the garlic
Keep together, do not part
It's time for the stake thro' the heart
Make no mistake, for this is war
My friend no less, no more.

A BIT OF WHAT YOU FANCY

Sitting by the log fire
Heart burning with desire
For a big roast spud
And a plate of Yorkshire pud.

SOUNDLESS

The sky is blacker than a raven's wing
Birds now no longer sing
Animals are cringing in fear
Why does this happen every year?
Tornadoes blanket the sky
Retribution from on high?
Destroying most things in its path
Is this God's vengeful wrath?
At last it's passed over
We can now leave our cover
Deadly quiet, no sound at all
You can hear a leaf fall
We are still alive, be grateful
Feel the silence engulf you.

WHAT IF IT RAINS?

At times my mind drifts to the past
When you said your love would last
Days when I would walk with pride
Because you were by my side.

Now I see flowers in the field gently sway
Even they cannot lift my sense of dismay
Sitting here by the phone
Alone, chilled to the bone
My number I think you've thrown away
Could have saved it for a rainy day.

MY GATE

Where I live the mail is always late
The postman doesn't know how to close a gate.

It's like being at the races
Put the horse thro' its paces
The gate was his first hurdle and he fell
Because he's only got one brain cell.

EDUCATION

Many a spell I have cast
Between future and past
Many a mind I have bound
New things you have found
Given you new things to do
Opened new avenues for you
Let you travel thro' the ages
Turn all of histories pages.

AUTUMN IN JUNE

Alone again at home waiting
For your call I'm praying
I only have photos of you
But my tears mar the view
My hair is now turning grey
It was black when you went away
There are words I long to hear
'Here I am, back home my dear.'
It's only spring I'm told
But the leaves seem to be turning gold
Only you can brighten this barren place
Bring a smile back to my face.

NEVER GIVE UP

No matter how far you are down
In life I have found
If you never give up hope
You can always cope.

LAST FLING

There are things I need to do in my life
Before I find myself a wife
Go out and have some fun
Before my life is completely undone.

FANTĂSY

If I could fly
With you on high
We could go away
Anywhere for a day
Hand in hand my love
Floating in the clouds above
Soar high over the sea
No earthy ties, completely free
Look at the beauty far below
Watch the mighty rivers flow
Colourful birds in the trees
See the oceans freeze
What a journey that would be
Together, just you and me.

TUNELESS

Floundering in a restless sea
Visions flashing before me
Eternally adrift on a loveless raft
Bitter sorrow such a chilling draught
Swirling around in an endless morass
Alone without a compass
Thoughts from an empty past float by
Screaming at a soulless sky
Lost on a desert island again
Love has such a bitter-sweet refrain.

FOOTPRINTS IN THE SAND

You are now full of sorrow
But I will give you back tomorrow
I will end your strife
Give you back your life
I will take you to a better place
Put a smile back on your face
Together we will walk hand in hand
And leave our footprints in the sand.

A DARKENED ROOM

Thought my mind was bound
With the love I had found
Thought it would last forever
But I wasn't being very clever
Heart broken in two
By my love for you
Why did you cause me so much pain
When you had nothing to gain?
In the dark at my table I sit
Although the room is brightly lit.

WAITING IN THE WINGS

The cat was teasing the mouse
Who once lived in the house
A voice said that's not nice
Attacking little mice
For you see the mouse had a mate
He was the guardian of the gate
As the friend started to growl
Thank you, screeched the owl
The dog's valiant efforts did not prevail
This is the end of a sad tail.

DERAILED

When I was young I was quite sporting
Rugby, football and boxing
Every day I would be out training
Even if it was raining.
I was good at all three
It was just second nature to me
In all three there was a career
But I went off the rails, hit the beer
Things that could have been
Ended by things I should have foreseen
I had the world at my feet
But my demons I could not beat.
To all you girls and boys
Do not fall for advertising ploys
If you want to succeed at sport
Drugs and booze you need to abort.
Who knows what you can achieve
If you just believe
Train hard, live clean
Don't end up like me, a has-been.

A STRANGER CAME CALLING

People should see me for what I am
For I am not a complex man
I am surrounded by fears
Shed my fair share of tears
But my heart is full of love
For I have been sent from above
To try to help people in need
Sow a loving seed
I am full of goodness you will find
If you will just give me time
I do magic tricks
Heal children who are sick
But please don't make a fuss
I'm but a poor man called Jesus.

LAZY MIND

I am not just a door
For I am more
To a mere mortal
I am but a portal
But outside my door
There's a whole world to explore.

UNISON

This shouldn't be
There's only me
Once we were one
Now you have gone
Oh how I long
Again to hear your song.

OH BOY

First time her lips touched mine
It was a feeling so divine
If this is the road to ecstasy
It's a place I long to be.

HAPPILY POOR

All my money is spent
And now I'm skint
But I'm quite content
Tho' my pockets are full of lint.

THE OLD CODGER

I've a sister called Mo
She's always ready to go
My nephew is Lee
He's the king bee
Steve is his brother's name
Ever ready for a game
I've also a cousin called Rita
You really should meet her
Me, I'm the codger losing his hair
They call me 'The grizzly old bear.'

ALLOTMENT

You rent a plot of land
Dig it over, spade in hand
With your sweat and toil
You prepare the soil
Raindrops on the earth fall
It's God's call
To water the seeds you sow
So your food can grow.

CUL DE SAC

It's really a shame
That you played your silly game
You had nothing to gain
By bringing me pain
You're going down a dead-end street
Nobody there for you to meet.

A DISTANT HORIZON

In my dreams my life is unravelling
Without hope, forever travelling
I'm by myself, always alone
Seeking a place to call home
Need an end to this quest
My mind cries out for a rest.

My life and dreams are the same
Oh I crave an end to this soulless game.

NATURE'S GIFT

Thro' my window I see daffodils in flower
They have unseen healing power
When I'm down and feeling low
I'm lifted by their lovely yellow glow.

WASH YOUR HANDS AFTER HANDLING

It comes from a huge hole
A piece of coal
It gives us light
And warmth at night.

BARMAID

I know a girl called Tia
Her middle name is Maria
For me she is always here
To bring me a cold beer.

HONEY

A busy bee buzzing by
Settled on a flower that caught his eye
I will 'bee' your best mate
If only you'll let me pollinate.

NO HUGS

I've built castles in the air
But no-one seemed to care
Never been asked if I have a dream
I don't matter it would seem.
Don't get hugs or kisses
No thoughts of my wishes
Need a shoulder to lay my head
Someone to end my fearful dread.

THE FORGETFUL POET

When words come to mind
Paper I need to find
Write them down before I forget
Just might be my best poem yet
I never throw a line away
Might come in handy one day.

ANTHEM

Why did it take so long to find
The answer to clear my mind
How to make myself heard
Just use the written word
My feelings I can now translate
Suppressed thoughts I can communicate
A way to show how I am feeling
Stop my mind from reeling.

Poems have been written thro' the ages
By lonely souls on many pages
But does anyone listen to them
Or will it be their final anthem
Will anyone really care?
That my soul I've laid bare
I don't know dear reader if you agree
But I thank you for listening to me.

LOVING WORDS

Your life I cannot live
But advice I can give
That's what dads are for
To give you love and more.
At times life can be tough
And things can get rough
But these things you can rise above
For I am here for you with love.
These words I want you to heed
Steer clear my children of greed
To yourself I say be true
And you always will come thro'

NIGHT CHILLS

Churning tide inside my mind
Answers I need to find
No pictures of your face
Need to feel your warm embrace
Miss you lying next to me
Oh how I miss your company
I need you here
To banish this lonely fear.

FREE AT LAST

Autumn's not far away
The skies are turning grey
There's a chill in the air
But why should you care
I suffered all your pain
All you gave me was rain
Didn't know how to cope
Tied in knots by your rope
But I have now cut myself free
At last ended your mystery
For now I have become wise
I can once again see the sunrise.

FEATHERBRAIN

A friend wanted a racing bird
Good pastime, so he had heard
But he wouldn't seek advice
Ah, this one looks nice
Talk about bad luck
Turned out it was a lame duck
Thought he had bought a racing pigeon
Turned out it was a skinny widgeon.

NO RESPITE

Into my life you were a light
A beacon in the night
I really did believe in you
But it was too good to be true
My concerns I tried to hide
Always smiling but inside I cried
Now I long for sleep
No longer to weep
Still I cannot hide my fears
In sleep I still shed tears.

DISH OF THE DAY

Pickled onions and cheese
You know how to please
Cheese and tomatoes on toast
A traditional Sunday roast
We cannot ever be apart
You've found the way to my heart.

SECOND TIME AROUND

On a cross he was nailed
Far below women wailed
Was his sacrifice really in vain
Did we learn, did we gain?
He said once more we'll hear his sweet refrain
When he comes to visit us again

Dark clouds of annihilation are crossing the horizon
Blocking out the light from the sun
There will be no place for neutrals
Armageddon doesn't play by known rules
World leaders do not show good behaviour
It's time for the return of the saviour.

FINALE

The old bear is getting weaker
As he does he becomes meeker
This winter will be his last
His die has now been cast
He stumbles back to his cave
It will soon be his grave.

CATASTROPHIC

The cat crept across the lawn
Thro' the mist of early dawn
He was out and about hunting
Should have read the bunting
For as he came out of the fog
There awaiting him was the dog.

Said the dog, 'Your lives are nine
But your chances today are not very fine
For I am hungry and have not ate
Come little kitty, caress my palate.'

HOPE SPRINGS ETERNAL

The flower beds feel the birth of spring
Blackbirds are starting to sing
The bees are leaving the hive
My senses are now coming alive
Daffodils in bud give my spirit a lift
This is nature's wondrous gift
A new love the earth has found
My optimism now does abound.

ITCHY FEET

Can't stay here anymore
New places to explore
Rucksack on my back
Get on the global track
Whole world before me
So much to see
Different peoples to meet
I've got wandering feet
New faces and places
Different foods and races.

NO HARD FEELINGS

This was not meant to be
You together with me
I know we tried to please
But we are chalk and cheese
Best we go our own way
Forget about today
What we had couldn't last
Time to leave it in the past.

REAL JOY

Kids, who would have them, hey!
They can do your head in each day
There are times you will seethe
But I say, just believe
To your life they will bring joy
Whether it's a girl or boy
Love for them you cannot deny
For on you they rely
On your face they will put a smile
They really make life worthwhile
Seeing their sweet innocent faces on the pillow
Makes you become all mellow.

ALWAYS

Whether I am far away over the sea
You will be there with me
Whatever I may say or do
Remember I will always love you.

BLACK COFFEE

Too long I've lived with my past
Seen the light at last
It's time again to mingle
My life to rekindle
For now I've stopped my alcoholic drinking
Because I was losing all my thinking
Causing everyone I love so much pain
Never would I see my children again.

It's been a very long rocky ride
But now I walk straight and with pride.

UNFORGIVING

In her warmth you will revel
But ignore her at your peril
For she can be mighty and strong
Does not know right from wrong
She can be an unruly child
Sometimes calm then wild
At times she can kill
So please don't doubt her will
She is a force to be reckoned with
For Mother Nature does not forgive.

EXCURSION

Young man seeking romance
Took the ferry to France
Ended up in a bar in Marseille
Nice place so they say
Needed work to pay his way
A place for him to stay
Got a job cleaning the streets
Enough to make ends meet
But it soon became a bore
Thinks he needs something more
Something to keep the blood coursing thro' his
veins
Not the same thing over and over again
He needs a real test
On his laurels he cannot rest
He doesn't need a job Nine-to-Five
Needs an adrenaline rush to keep his senses alive
Ended up in the Djibouti region
Serving in the French Foreign Legion.

WELCOME TO THE REAL WORLD

I knew one day you would fly the nest
Enter the big world, give it a test
You and your boyfriend in your first home together
Hope your new life has clement weather
You now have your own bills to pay
Take your time, feel your way.
I know you have great merit
And won't buy things on credit
Problems you can rise above
Because you have so much love
But if the rent is overdue
Remember I am here for you.

SLEEPLESS

I try my best to sleep
But thoughts awaken from the deep
For my mind is whirling
The kraken is now stirring
Things that were buried inside
I can no longer hide
Feelings I thought were in the past
Should have known that wouldn't last
It was a spell over me you cast
Then you nailed me to your mast.

LOST AND FOUND

Sunday morning walk in the park
Sit at home in the dark
Look at the sky above
Where are you my love?
I would write you a letter
But I think I know better
Birds sing in the trees
You brought me to my knees
There's a light in the sky
A message from on high
Apologies are now too late
I've found another mate.

DAMSELFLY

In a hot summer's sky
I see the delicate little damselfly
Skimming across the water as they fly
Creatures of beauty, pleasing to the eye.

BLUSHING

Just the touch of your hands
My feelings leapt out of bounds
Senses were sent reeling
What is this feeling?
Things are stirring deep inside
So much turmoil inside my mind
Emotions I've not felt before
Please don't close the door
This is a beautiful trend
Oh please let it never end.

REFLECTIONS

Sunshine rippling across the sea
Won't bring you nearer to me
The moon shining over 'our' lake
Makes my grieving heart ache
Laughing children on a summer's day
Cannot take my pain away
Rain falling on the windowpane
Leave images of your face again
But were they the image of you
Or just my tears blurring the view?
The happy times we had together
Are memories that will last forever
Whatever I do in the rest of my life
You will always be my best friend, my wife.

A NEVER-ENDING LOVE

I'm involved in a deep romance
With Cornwall and Penzance
A place of so much beauty
It really is God's own country
So many charming places to see
The whole area fascinates me
The pasties you cannot beat
Such a simple scrumptious treat
The year I spent there was so nice
I thought I was in paradise.

BEST FRIEND

Together you go for a walk
You are both quiet, no need to talk
Back home lying by the fire they will laze
Giving you such a loving gaze
They are so beautiful and caring
All their love they are sharing
Of your life they are a major part
A loving being with a big heart
The best friend you will ever find
They have four legs and are called a canine.

A REFRESHING BREEZE

Where do you start and I begin
Thought we were one, you my twin
Running thro' fields of green
The two of us in a dream
When I thought things were fine
A message came down the line.

Sitting alone, seething in my mind
Got to get out, take a ride
Feel the breeze on my face
Find a happier place
Put you in the bin of my past
Rejoin the human race at last.

MEDIUM RARE

It's a hot summer's day
You need to take the heat away
Take a swim in the pool
A good way to keep cool
Come out, sit in the sun
Take the rays but don't get overdone
Put on plenty of sun lotion
But make sure it's the right potion.

WORLD THRO' MY EYES

No one can understand me
Thro' my eyes they cannot see
They have not been where I have been
Seen the things I have seen
If they could go thro' my mind
A better world they would try to find
If they would just stop and think
Don't let their minds blink
They could make a better tomorrow
End all the pain and sorrow.

POLITICAL PRISONER

You can take my freedom away
But I'll be a free man one day
For I've walked down the track
Been put on the rack
Taken all of life's pain
Shaken off the snow and rain
So you will soon find
You cannot take my mind
Though I may be from a different region
My politics are not based on religion
Although I'm chained and bound
My head is high, I remain unbowed.

A TICKING CLOCK

We are going on a trip to the stars
Plot the course, destination Mars
For we have to find a new place
To re-house the Human Race.
Our sun will explode in a huge nuclear blast
Consigning Planet Earth to histories past.
Mankind cannot travel light years away
Floating around in a spaceship day after day
We may still be able to speak
But our bodies will be very weak.
So one thing is a priority
We must create artificial gravity.
Religion will be banned because it creates wars
We cannot export that to the stars
Then we can live in peace and love
High in the stars above.
The human race needs to lift its pace
If it wants to become a galactic race
Supply ships will be the first to go
Until our own food we can grow
But first we will need volunteers
To become the new pioneers.

WHAT IF?

You jump in the shower
Turn on the power
You wash and scrub
Jump in the hot tub
But if we had pyjamas that cleansed us at night
That would be such a lovely delight
Wake up, change and off to school
Always looking fresh and cool.

FATAL EXTRACTION

Here I am in the dentist's chair
Mind bubbling over in fear
Don't want to be here
Prefer to be sipping a beer.

I told her my teeth are fine
We've been friends a long time
But my senses she's trying to lull
Think she fancies me, she's on the pull.

REVEAL ALL

So you are another year older
That's no reason to look younger
To you I make this plea
Please share your secret with me
Why don't you grow graceful with age
Or haven't you read that page?

HOT AND HUMID

It was a hot summer's night
My heart leapt with delight
All our clothes were gone
You and I united as one
Sexual chemistry a beautiful mixture
Do you fancy a return fixture?

NOT OF THIS WORLD

For years astronomers have searched space
Looking for signs of an alien race
They say there are no worlds like earth
We've searched for all our worth.
But alien life on earth is here
They have been for many a year.
For our lives they make the rules
Treat us all as fools
While they do just as they please
They think there's no one to appease
But the people have now found
Their greed will not be bound
At the trough to their hearts' content
We call them Members of Parliament.

A COOL REFRESHING DRINK

Have a drink of beer
It can bring you cheer
Help you cool down
Remove that frown
But don't drink to drown your sorrow
The pain will still be there tomorrow.

MORNING VISITORS

I throw the seed across the lawn
Now I wait for early dawn
The seed is not for the grass
But for any bird that may pass
By the window I now sit
Who will be first, a sparrow or blue tit?
Their song I love to hear
To my soul they bring cheer.

NOT OUT

When I was young and in my clover
I once bowled a maiden over
But she had me leg before wicket
I thought, this isn't cricket!

Something a little different, a little story:

TOO HARD

'You're too hard on him sometimes.'

'What yer mean I'm too hard on him, he's eight years old for goodness sake.' I says turning over to face her: 'Oh gaud, I wish you wouldn't wear your curlers in bed sweetheart.'

'Never mind my curlers, you're too hard on him telling him there's no Father Christmas.'

'Look, I've a lot of early morning deliveries to make tomorrow and I can't spend all night arguing with you.

Good night Mrs Claus.'

And finally

AU REVOIR

To anybody out there
Who may care
This old bear
Is now going off the air.

ND - #0520 - 270225 - C0 - 203/127/7 - PB - 9781861510488 - Matt Lamination